The Business of You: Eliminating Money Blocks

Table of Contents

"Money isn't the most important thing in life, but it's reasonably close to oxygen on the 'gotta have it' scale."
- ZIG ZIGLAR

INTRODUCTION

What are money blocks? **Money blocks are beliefs and behaviors that limit your ability to earn and/or keep money.**

Everyone has money blocks. Even a billionaire can have them. There's a reason why they don't have even more money, and many billionaires would like another billion. They didn't get that way on accident. Money was a priority for them. Their money blocks are just less limiting than those of most of us.

Money blocks can take a variety of forms, but beliefs and behaviors are the most common. Some examples of each include:

Beliefs

- "Earning money is too hard."
- "I'm too old to become wealthy."
- "It's too late for me to save enough money for retirement."
- "I won't have any free time if I make earning money a priority."
- "The taxes will kill me."
- "Good people don't care about money."
- "People won't like me anymore."
- "I don't deserve it."

- "I'm not enough."
- "People like me never get ahead."
- "This is the best job I can possibly get."
- Fear of success
- Fear of failure

Behaviors

- Overspending
- Procrastinating
  - This can be related to paying bills on time or waiting to begin saving for retirement or looking for a better job.
- Poor financial priorities
- Exercising excessive generosity

A lack of knowledge can also be a money block. If you want to invest your money, but don't know anything about investing, you're blocked from investing successfully.

Money blocks can keep you from earning, saving, and investing money wisely. **Money blocks can prevent you from even believing these things are possible for you.** Money blocks have the power to wreck your finances and your financial future.

Money blocks can be deep-seated or simple to change, depending on the particular block. One thing is for certain: they're unlikely to leave on their own, and it's your responsibility to deal with them if you wish to make more money.

> "Finance is not merely about making money. It's about achieving our deep goals and protecting the fruits of our labor. It's about stewardship and, therefore, about achieving the good society."
> *- ROBERT J. SHILLER*

Consider these topics to learn more about your money blocks and your opportunities for success:

1. **Chapter 1: Sources of Money Blocks.** Money blocks can come from several different sources. Do you know the origin of yours? Understanding the sources of money blocks will demonstrate how pervasive they can be.

2. **Chapter 2: Releasing Money Blocks.** Money blocks can take more than one form, but the method for dealing with them is similar. Whether your block is a belief, habit, or other behavior, you'll learn how to address it.

3. **Chapter 3: Try a 30-Day Challenge.** Does making a permanent change sound too intimidating for you? The answer is a 30-day challenge. A month isn't a long time, but you can accomplish more than you think.

4. **Chapter 4: Affirmations.** Positive affirmations about money tackle your money blocks by changing your thoughts. They can make a huge difference. Changing your thoughts also changes your beliefs and actions that precede and follow your thoughts.

5. **Chapter 5: How to Prepare Your Children for Financial Abundance.** Maybe you got the short end of the stick in your childhood as it relates to money blocks. You can avoid doing the same to your children. Use this information to help your children thrive financially.

"All the breaks you need in life wait within your imagination. Imagination is the workshop of your mind, capable of turning mind energy into accomplishment and wealth."
- NAPOLEON HILL

SOURCES OF MONEY BLOCKS

There are many sources of money blocks. Many of them might be a surprise to you.

Understanding the many sources of money blocks will show you how long you've been struggling with them.

It will also demonstrate the importance of keeping yourself aware of when you may be facing a potential new money block.

Money blocks are created from a variety of sources:

1. **Family upbringing.** Everyone has money blocks, including your parents. **You may have many of the same money blocks they do.** Unless you were incredibly fortunate to be born with parents that had a minimal number of money blocks, you have some work to do.

   - It's unlikely that your family made a point of teaching you an abundance mindset. This oftentimes is due to your family's lack of knowledge regarding abundance.

- Most "polite" people avoid talking about money and money management. It's considered a taboo topic whether the discussion happens at home with loved ones or outside the home with strangers.

2. **Religion.** Many religions, intentionally and unintentionally, consider money as bad. The poor are held in rather high regard.

    - Wealth is commonly viewed as an obstacle to faith and enlightenment. Even a middle-class lifestyle is viewed as excessive in some religions.

    - Studies have shown that those who place a high priority on religion often feel uncomfortable and guilty if they are financially well off.

3. **Low self-esteem.** Feelings of self-worth and self-esteem aren't always easy to come by. Unless you were successful as a child and had parents that made a point of building these qualities in you, you could probably use a boost.

    - Unless you actively work on these traits, your money blocks will continue to affect your financial life.

- **If you feel unworthy of success and comfort, those things will prove elusive.**

4. **Guilt.** Most of us are good people. It can be challenging to drive around in a car that costs $100,000 without any guilt. After all, you could instead house several homeless families with that money and drive a 5-year-old Honda Civic instead.

    - This is a personal decision. **At the very least, eliminating your money blocks would allow you to attract more abundance and help more people.**

    - There's a difference between self-love and narcissism. There's a difference between being happy with yourself and lacking empathy for others. You can hold yourself in high regard and still care about others. As adults, we're each responsible for our own success in life.

5. **A fear of success.** Success is attractive, but at the same time, it's not for most people. We've been taught to fit in and conform. Our school years teach us that being just like everyone else is the comfortable place to be.

    - Most of us are wary of having power and the responsibility that comes with it.

- We also don't want to be noticed too much. We want a little attention, but not a lot. It feels safer and more comfortable to be inconspicuous.

- If you're going to be "big" in life, it requires dealing with attention and responsibility.

6. **The media.** Whether you're watching the news or a movie on Saturday night, the financially strapped are portrayed as the underdog. The wealthy person or company is often considered the villain.

Money blocks come from a variety of forms. What do you think was the primary source of yours?

Only a few people possess the right mindset, beliefs, and behaviors to build and maintain wealth. Luckily, even though it may take some work, you can undo your money blocks and move toward prosperity.

"Keep your dreams alive.
Understand to achieve anything
requires faith and belief in
yourself, vision, hard work,
determination, and dedication.
Remember all things are possible
for those who believe."
- GAIL DEVERS

RELEASING MONEY BLOCKS

Clearing money blocks requires a multifaceted strategy. **It's important to address beliefs, habits, and assumptions.** Each of these can be attacked from a variety of angles. It's a lot of work but consider the payoff that lies ahead.

When you greatly reduce your number and severity of money blocks, anything becomes possible. With money blocks, becoming wealthy is like running a marathon with a broken leg - painful and unlikely.

Beliefs

Your beliefs form the foundation of your abundance mindset. Your beliefs can vary from "I don't have what it takes to be wealthy" to "I'll have plenty of time when I'm older to save money." Money blocks at this level affect your ability to create and hold wealth more than any other type of block.

Your beliefs influence your decisions, actions, and habits. These are the things that ultimately determine whether you become financially successful.

Perhaps the most important step in this journey is to create a compelling future. **When you know where you want to go, it's easier to identify your money blocks.** The person that wants to live the life of a jet set billionaire doesn't have all the same money blocks as someone that truly just wants to live in a three-bedroom ranch in Cheboygan.

There's no right or wrong answer but figure out what kind of life you want to live. Be able to describe it in detail. Painting a picture of the kind of life you want to live will enable to you determine if having a certain amount of money is necessary in order to achieve your goals.

Use these strategies to change your beliefs and your financial future:

1. **Identify your beliefs.** Look at every belief you have about money - good or bad - and write them down. You should end up with quite a long list.

   - Take at least 60 minutes to do this. Then, spend a few minutes each day for the next several days adding to your list. New ideas will come to you.

- Be expansive in your consideration. Don't look at just obvious beliefs. Look at beliefs you have regarding success and achievement, too. Your overall philosophy of life could be a source of money blocks.

2. **Determine which blocks are harming you the most.** Look over your list of beliefs and ask yourself, "Which of these beliefs is limiting my financial health the most?" Listen to the response you get.

   - Create a Top-10 list of your negative beliefs. **It's important to attack the most crucial beliefs first,** so figure out which are causing you the most harm.

3. **Examine the belief.** Choose the most harmful belief and examine it. Begin by identifying the source of the block.

   - "How did I acquire this belief?"

   - Where did you get this belief? Did you acquire it as a child from your own powers of reasoning? Is it something you gleaned from TV? Parents? Did you get it from a fictional movie or book? Did it come from church?

4. **Consider the quality of the source.** Is your Aunt Betty really a great source of financial wisdom? How successful is the person that gave you this idea? Is a

fictional story the best place to acquire a belief?

- "Is the source of this belief reliable?"

5. **Consider the intention of the source.** If you were told by someone that this belief was a good idea, ask yourself what their intention was. Were they trying to help you or limit you? Did they have your best interests at heart?

6. **Question the validity of the belief.** Upon close examination, you might find that the belief isn't true.

- Is it possible this belief isn't true? Why or why not?

7. **What is this belief costing you?** Make a list of all the challenges and negative outcomes that result from this belief. The longer the list the better.

8. **Create a new, positive belief.** What is a new belief that serves you in your quest to attain wealth? Here are few examples:

- Old belief: "It doesn't matter if I pay my bills on time. It's only an extra $30 if I'm late."

- New belief: "$30 invested today is worth over a thousand dollars in the future. There's no reason to waste money. It only takes a few minutes to pay my bills on time."

- Old belief: "Earning a lot of money takes too much time."

- New belief: "If I make enough money, I'll have all the free time in world. Besides, by prioritizing my time, I can make plenty of money and still have time for the important things in my life."

9. **Try out the new belief in your life.** There are few things certain in life. Life is more of an experiment. Approaching life with this attitude makes it more enjoyable and interesting. It's also easier to try new beliefs and behaviors. It doesn't have to be a permanent change; **you can just experiment.**

   - Give yourself <u>90 days</u> to try out a new way of approaching the world with your new belief. Just try it. You can always go back or try something else. What do you have to lose?

   - You already know that what you're currently doing isn't working. Take a chance on something that might work.

10. **Make the belief part of you.** Always keep a list of your new beliefs with you. A small notebook or your smartphone is perfect. Look at your list of new, positive beliefs several times each day. Read your list to yourself in bed in the morning and evening. Any other times would be a bonus.

11. **Act as if.** Our beliefs change to explain our behavior. **When you act in a new way, your beliefs change to accommodate that behavior.** It's too uncomfortable otherwise.

   - If you start acting like $10 matters, you'll begin to believe that $10 matters.

   - If you save money from each paycheck for a couple of months, you'll believe that saving is important.

   - If you study investing each day for a few minutes, you'll believe that you can build an understanding of investing.

Beliefs form the foundation of behavior. **Identifying and changing one belief can change numerous behaviors.** You get a lot of bang for your buck when you address your beliefs. Keep this in mind.

"Of the billionaires I have known, money just brings out the basic traits in them. If they were jerks before they had money, they are simply jerks with a billion dollars."
- Warren Buffet

Behaviors and Habits

After addressing your beliefs, it's necessary to look at your behaviors and habits. **Beliefs influence the actions you take, and it's your consistent actions that determine your long-term results.** This statement is true in every aspect of your life, not just the financial aspects of your life.

This means that you likely have some habits you'll want to eliminate and others you'll want to build. The process of modifying your behaviors and habits is like modifying your beliefs. It all starts with identification.

These techniques will help you to change your behaviors:

1. **Identify your behaviors that affect your finances.** Some of these are obvious, while others are more challenging to identify. If you've never thought about it, there are plenty of things you do that you don't realize affect your finances. Think carefully.

   - **Saving.** What are your current behaviors and habits around saving money? How much of your paycheck do you currently save? How easy is it for you to take money out of your savings and spend it on something unnecessary? In order to answer this question, you must have a realistic understanding of the term necessary versus unnecessary.

- **Earning.** Do you have any behaviors or habits that can lead to increased earnings? For example, do you spend some time each week looking for a better job? Do you research investment opportunities? Are you building websites on the weekend to sell or lease?

- **Spending.** How much money do you spend that you don't need to spend? How do you make spending decisions? Do you go out to eat a lot? Do you buy coffee at Starbucks instead of making it at home? Do you buy things you don't really need?

- **Investing.** How do you make investing decisions? Do you take stock tips from your butcher? Are you conservative or aggressive? Do you invest in things you understand?

- **Giving.** How much do you spend on gifts? Do you loan money to friends? How much do you give to charity (a church is a charity) ? Does the amount of money you give away impact your finances significantly? How do you decide how much to give?

- **Leisure time.** You might wonder how your leisure time is relevant but remember that is time that you can spend however you like. Is that time being spent in a way that helps or harms your finances? Are you using that time wisely?

2. **Identify changes that you want to make.** Everyone's time is limited. Spend your time on the behaviors that are going to make the biggest difference in your life.

   - **Identify the five most important behaviors you want to change.** Think about both short and long term. Imagine the impact that making this behavioral change will have on your life in a month and over 10 years.

3. **Make a list of the benefits of making this change.** Give your brain some good reasons for making this change. Imagine that you wanted to create a habit of saving 10% of your income:

   - It would help to cover emergencies, such as a new furnace.

   - It would give peace of mind. It's not always easy to sleep at night with little savings.

- It would eventually result in saving thousands of dollars.

- Retirement would be more enjoyable and stress free.

- You could help others with some of the money.

- You could take that trip to Rome you've dreamt about for the last decade.

4. **Start small. Make a small change and build upon it.** For example, you could start by saving 1% of your paycheck and save an additional percent each month or each paycheck until you've reached your goal.

5. **Interrupt your thinking before taking a negative action.** For example, suppose you're about to spend money. Rather than just spend it without further thought, you might follow a new pattern:

   - Ask yourself, "Is this something I need?"

   - "Why do I want to buy this?"

   - "How much money will this cost me over 20 or 30 years? Use a financial calculator online.

   - What could I do instead of spending this money?

- If you still want to spend it, you might require yourself to wait a week and re-gauge your interest.

6. **Reward yourself for compliance. Behaviors that are rewarded tend to recur.** Obviously, it's important to be careful about spending too much money as a form of reward. Find something that will make it a little more worth your while to change your behavior.

7. **Be patient.** Many of our behaviors are to avoid discomfort in one form or another. By changing your behavior, you're likely to feel uncomfortable. Be strong but be patient with yourself. Change can take time.

Your behaviors are where the rubber meets the road. **Your actions create the results you experience in your life.** Your beliefs influence your behaviors. Your behaviors build your life.

"I always knew I was going to be rich. I don't think I ever doubted it for a minute."
- WARREN BUFFETT

TRY A 30-DAY CHALLENGE

A 30-day challenge can be a powerful way to alter your thinking and behavior. **It's easy to get started on something that only lasts for 30 days.** Making a long-term change is much more intimidating. Getting started is half the battle, so a 30-day challenge has a big advantage.

In essence, you're going to try a new behavior for the next 30 days. For many people, this is long enough to create a new habit. Some people require a bit more but it's a great start, nonetheless. It's also long enough to judge if the behavior is helpful to you.

Imagine the impact of doing twelve 30-day challenges each year. Not only would it keep life interesting, but you'd make some incredible changes, especially as the years added up!

Use this process to try an effective 30-day challenge:

1. **Choose wisely.** What will be the focus of the next 30 days? Avoid spending too much time on this. If you've made it this far, you know where you need some work. Pick something and get started.

- Take on something challenging, but not too brutal. **Give yourself a great opportunity to be successful.** It's human nature to want to push things to the limit, but the words "extreme" and "progress" rarely go together. Don't underestimate the power in incremental change over time.

- Be sure to choose something beneficial. The years are passing by, so make the most of the next month.

- What will your challenge be? What benefits do you expect to gain?

2. **Define your objective clearly.** Know what success will look like. It shouldn't be questionable.

   - "Spend less money" is not well-defined.
   - "Bring my lunch to work each day" is easy to measure and interpret.

3. **Figure out the potential obstacles.** If you know where the challenges lie, you can prepare for them in advance. Let's stick with our "bring lunch to work each day" example. What are the potential obstacles?

   - Not having food at home to pack

- Dealing with Jim - we go out to lunch at least three times each week.

- I need to get out of the office during lunch to preserve my mental health.

- I don't have a good way to carry my lunch to work.

What are some possible solutions?

- Go to the grocery store every Sunday and buy enough for the week.

- Have Jim meet you at the park for lunch, and he can carry his food out. Explain to him what you're doing. Encourage him to do the same.

- Eat at the park. Eat at the mall. Eat in your car. Eat at your desk and then take off for 30 minutes.

- Buy an adult lunch box or small cooler.

4. **Generate enthusiasm.** Get yourself psyched up. **Imagine how great it will feel** to show yourself that you have enough control to change your behavior. Think of the benefits you'll gain. Remind yourself that it's only 30 days. You can do it!

5. **Have a plan for dealing with a bad day.** Bad days happen to everyone. There will be a day you want to

cheat on your 30-day challenge. Just do your best and keep going.

- Tell yourself that you're going to stick with it today, but you can cheat tomorrow if you still really want to. You'll be likely to survive another day, and tomorrow you'll likely feel better without having to resort to cheating.

- If you do slip one day, avoid feeling too bad about it. Twenty-nine days out of 30 is still a pretty good average!

6. **Evaluate.** Evaluate how things are going throughout the 30 days. What can you do to make the process easier? Where are your sticking points?

   - Finally, evaluate your results. Is this something that would be worthwhile to continue?

   - Does it give you ideas for additional 30-day challenges?

A 30-day challenge can create significant change in a hurry. It's only 30 days, so you can do it! **You're free to go back to the way things were before, but you won't.** Give a 30-day challenge a test-run.

> "Wealth is the ability to fully experience life."
> - Henry David Thoreau

AFFIRMATIONS

Affirmations are familiar to everyone, but few people actually use them consistently, if they use them at all. **Affirmations take time to create results, but you can't help but be influenced by positive messages you read, speak, and hear over and over again.** It's a simple, non-threatening tool that can really help.

Effective affirmations share several characteristics, such as:

1. **Positive.** Avoid stating affirmations in the negative. Your brain doesn't work that way, and you'll get unreliable results. For example:

   - Not this way: I don't spend money that I don't have to spend.

- Yes, say this: I only spend money when necessary.

- Not this way: I am no longer a poor person.
- Yes, say this: I am becoming wealthier each day.

2. **Present tense.** Avoid the words will, was, have been, and so on.

   - If you say, "I will be wealthy," you're never going to be wealthy. You're always going to be in the stage before wealth.

   - Instead, say, "I am wealthy."

3. **Simple.** The part of your brain we're addressing is powerful, but simple. Avoid confusing it.

   - Avoid: I am comfortable with wealth, and I like to save money and invest it to the best of my ability.

   - Keep it super simple. Pick one thought: I am comfortable with wealth.

   - A 2nd affirmation could be: I like to save money.

   - A 3rd affirmation could be: I invest wisely.

Now that you know how to create an effective affirmation, choose an area of your financial life and create 5-10 affirmations that will help you. Better yet, create or look up a huge list of affirmations and choose 5-10 that work for you.

When using affirmations, avoid these common affirmation errors:

1. **Too many.** Affirmations require repetition. You can't repeat 300 affirmations very many times each day. How many is too many? More than ten.

2. **Too few.** It's hard to know if a particular affirmation will stick, so avoid limiting yourself to just one. Pick one area you'd like to work on, such as saving, and create several related affirmations. Five to 10 works well.

3. **A lack of focus.** Rather than have one affirmation on saving, one on investing, one on spending, and so on, choose one area of focus.

4. **A lack of consistency.** Affirmations require a lot of repetition. Morning, noon, and night are good starts. **It's important to say them daily.**

5. **A lack of patience.** It's going to take time. It's only a few minutes each day, so you have little to lose. Expect it to take months to see benefits and be

pleasantly surprised when it takes less.

6. **A lack of visualization.** Words alone are not enough. Instead of just telling yourself, "I like to save money," imagine saving money and how great it feels. **Your brain likes pictures and feelings,** so give it some to work with.

Affirmation errors are critical in nature. Any one of these errors is enough to make your efforts a waste of time. Double check all your affirmations and how you use them in your life.

Now that you have a list of affirmations and know the common errors, let's make a plan for implementing affirmations into your life.

Try these techniques to be successful with affirmations:

1. **Put your list of affirmations into multiple formats.** Put them on your phone, write them down, and record them so you can listen to them. Keep them handy with a variety of formats.

2. **Write your affirmations at least once each day.** Put them in a notebook so you can keep track of them each day. <u>Write them out by hand</u>. Typing into a word processor doesn't work as well.

3. **Read your affirmations for at least five minutes each day.** Just keep reading the list over and over. Ideally, you will do this aloud for half of the time and silently for the other half.

    - Repeat this five-minute routine at least twice each day.

4. **Listen to your affirmations as much as possible:** In the car, waiting in line, and lying in bed. Listen as much as you can stand.

    - **Right before sleeping and right after waking up are the most effective times.** Avoid having your affirmations play while you're asleep. Studies show that it doesn't help and can disturb your sleep.

5. **Remember to visualize.** You don't have to lie down in a trance but have a picture in your mind for each affirmation as you repeat them.

That's it! This makes for a great 30-day challenge, too. It only requires a few minutes each day and will work if you put in the time and effort.

Create a few affirmations and see what happens. What do you have to lose? Use them daily and watch what happens. Be patient and you'll be sure to see positive results.

"It's the repetition of affirmations that leads to belief. And once that belief becomes a deep conviction, things begin to happen."
- *MUHAMMAD ALI*

HOW TO PREPARE YOUR CHILDREN FOR FINANCIAL ABUNDANCE

You now know the basics of money blocks. You know about a compelling future, beliefs, poor behaviors, habits, and affirmations. How can you use this to help your children avoid the negative effects of money blocks?

Fortunately, you can do a lot for them!

Most importantly, **give them the beliefs about money and wealth they need to thrive financially.** Avoid any talk or behavior that will limit them. Watch your words and behaviors around them.

- Avoid foolish spending.
- Show them how you save money.
- Explain the ideas of abundance, consistent work, and a positive attitude.
- Have regular talks with them about money.
- Work hard to build their self-esteem and confidence.

Your children are always watching and listening. Set a good example for them and you'll be happy with the results.

They might even thank you someday.

"All money is a matter of belief."
- ADAM SMITH

CONCLUSION

Money blocks can take many forms. Your beliefs, attitudes, behaviors, and knowledge base can be money blocks. A dead-end job can be a money block if you stick with it. Think of a money block as anything that inhibits your ability to build and maintain financial wealth.

Money blocks are acquired from a variety of sources. Your parents and upbringing are the biggest source of money blocks, but you may have also made incorrect judgements of the world based on your own reasoning and experiences. TV, books, and other sources of media can also be sources of money blocks.

Addressing your limiting beliefs can be the most effective way to deal with money blocks, because changing a single belief can alter multiple behaviors. Beliefs have far reaching consequences.

Self-esteem is another area of major importance. If you doubt your capabilities or your worthiness, you're going to struggle with building wealth. You'll sabotage your efforts if you can even get started in the first place.

If you strive to prosper but get lackluster results, you likely have money blocks. Overcome these blocks and you'll be on an exciting journey to claim the financial abundance you deserve.